YOUR DESTINY IN MOTION

WORKBOOK

BY GEORGE BISSETT

A Process Of Self – Evaluation

DEDICATION

This book is dedicated to my three daughters – Dorothy, Terri, and Lynette – and their families. Just because.

ACKNOWLEDGEMENTS

Bob Bray is my friend and business partner; Bob and his wife, Dawn, motivated me to write out what I had so many times talked to them about. If you check out our website (www.dynamicdiscovery.ca) you will see that Bob has excellent 'helping" skills of his own.

I have gained much fun and insight from my Saturday morning "breakfast club" members; Gord, Mannie, Mike, Bob, and Cliff. These guys are both hilarious and wise at the same time. Thanks for the stories and support. And I apologize for all the times I skipped out when it was my turn to pay – but there will be no reimbursement.

And heartfelt thanks to Christina (Chrissy) Rice who has organized and formatted my words and has been the driving force behind getting this book published.

Table Of Contents

Exercise 1

Exercise 2

Concept of Change

Speedometer

How the Mind Works

Punishment or Reward?

Relationships and Behavior

Relationships and Needs

Control Car

Control Computer

Goal Setting

Live Up To Your Greatest Potential

Focus On Your Potential

Futurizing (Having our world the way we want it to be)

DGS (darn good start)

The Process

How It Works

Conclusion

Personal Inventory Guide

Resources

About The Author

Disclaimer

FORWARD

What do you really want from life? An improved career? More money? A happy marriage? A new home? Fame? Success? Whatever it is, you can have it. No matter whether it seems impossible right now.

Imagine the life of your dreams…and make it come true through the ***Destiny in Motion*** process; a process that will help you harness your own power of positive thinking, stress management, instinct and, above all, commitment.

The ***Destiny in Motion*** process will show you how to conceive, believe and achieve the goals you truly desire. With an open mind and dedication, you will quickly learn how to literally have everything you want. The *Destiny in Motion* process will give you the insight and knowledge you need to reach your goals.

PLEASE note that you will encounter several references to Best Interest so the following is a description of that concept:

- Best Interest is proposed as a positive way to manage your life. Whatever it is you're planning to do, ask yourself if it is intended to help you or hurt another.

But there is another way of assessing yourself, so let's look at that:

- Whatever it is you're planning to do, ask yourself this: Would I still do (this) if I knew that my family and friends would see me doing (this)?
- If your answer to the Alternative approach question is "No" then you should ask yourself this: Am I being hypocritical by wanting to do things that I'm ashamed or fearful that those closest to me will find out about?
- Then ask yourself what is wrong with what you're intending to do that requires it to be kept secret? Write your answer below:

_____

_____

Visit our web site http://dynamicdiscovery.ca/ for more information about us.

Your Destiny In Motion Workbook

INTRODUCTION

This is a program about balancing home, social, work activities and relationships. *"Your Destiny in Motion"* is about getting what you really, really, <u>really</u> want from your life.

A balanced life is certainly an achievable goal… **if**:

- you really, really, <u>really</u> want balance
- you are willing to do <u>anything</u> to get balance

TO BE SUCCESSFUL WE NEED FAITH & A CAUSE

For now, all you need is an open mind. Don't worry about taking notes as everything you will need is in this book. You <u>will</u> remember the material because there is no pressure and no test. No pass or fail. This is a logical process, not a theoretical proposition.

In our Dynamic Discovery workshops, we use a couple simple exercises to illustrate the power and inventiveness of the human mind.

The following two exercises illustrate how the qualities of the 5 senses work. You will be asked to make a picture in your mind (an internal representation). For some people, the pictures they make in their minds are very clear. For others, the picture is not clear, and yet they may have a sense of it being there and if they were asked questions about its qualities they would be able to give an answer. To keep the exercises simple, we will only work with visual memories.

EXERCISE 1:

Get in a comfortable position, close your eyes and get a picture in your mind of someone you really enjoy being with. When you get this picture, notice:

- Is it the picture bright or dim?
  _____

- Where is it located – are you inside or outside?
  _____

- Do you have other observations?
  _____
  _____
  _____

- Once you have done this, open your eyes and clear your mind by stretching and looking around the room.

Again close your eyes and this time get a picture in your mind of someone you do not enjoy being with. Notice the emotions attached to this picture and I am sure that you can identify several that are different from the picture of someone you enjoy being with. Once you have done this, break state by stretching and looking around the room.

I am sure you were able to identify several thoughts and feelings that were different in the two internal representations. Record those thoughts here:

_____

_____

_____

_____

Generally, we tend to have similar thoughts and feelings for the internal representations of people we enjoy being with. The thoughts and feelings of the internal representations of people we do not enjoy being with will also be similar but different. This sameness and difference in thoughts and feelings allows us to code our experiences and give meaning to our past and future memories (internal representations).

Images of our thoughts and feelings are fun and easy to play with. For example, if the internal representation of someone you do not enjoy being with is large, and up close (that is, right in your face), what do you think would happen if you made the picture smaller and pushed it away to a comfortable distance? I suspect you would not necessarily end up liking this person, however you may find them to be not so overbearing.

EXERCISE 2:

For this exercise, I would like you to get comfortable in your chair, close your eyes, and think of a time when you were very happy. Once you have this picture, make it very dark, shrink it down to a small picture and push it far away.

- When you did this, what happened? Did your feelings of happiness reduce or disappear?

  _____
  _____

You have just learned a great way to <u>remove</u> happiness from your life, and that is to take all your happy memories and make the pictures very dark, small and far away. Although this is a negative exercise its value is in demonstrating the power of your mind and explains the unhappiness of some people and how they tend to discount their happy memories by making them darker, smaller and further away, while making their unpleasant memories big and bright and close. They do that and then live their lives in a state of unhappiness.

These two examples illustrate that attaching images to your stored memories (past and present) give meaning to those memories. We cannot change an event that has already happened, however by adjusting the images of the memory we can change how we perceive it and respond to it. This is also true for future events.

In our *Dynamic Discovery workshops*, the Leader will usually posit a statement then ask the group two questions that are very similar to what has been asked before. The statement is:

- You go to sleep tonight and a miracle happens. All the advances in your life and your community that you hope to happen have taken place. The miracle happens while you are asleep so you don't actually know that it has happened.

The questions are:

When you wake up in the morning, what is the first thing that you <u>will</u> notice *you are doing* that <u>will</u> tell you the miracle has happened?

_____

_____

_____

_____

What next?

_____

_____

_____

_____

See if you can place yourself into the "questions", bearing in mind that problems are often defined in terms of what others do, situations that you might not feel you have influence over. That is why your emphasis must be on what will be <u>different</u> about *yourself* because you do have the power to change that. Having a clear vision of what will be different, and that you know you have the power to change, is a significant step towards actually bringing it about.

By making the questions as open as possible, it is much more likely that the answers that come out of an actual workshop will be grounded in the group members own experiences, yet will encompass endless possibilities. Notice that the question is specifically <u>not</u> about changed circumstances due to some magic, but what you (and the other participants, if any) would be *doing* differently.

We tend to think of problems / difficulties as being ahead of us, and forget about the problems that have already been solved by our efforts.

Let that sink in...

We often do not acknowledge that we have a history of solving problems and, instead, focus on our seeming inability to solve other problems. If focus leads to obsession then those unsolved problems overwhelm us.

The lesson here is that it is sometimes of value to give ourselves credit so as to come to accept that we are capable of dealing with our problems – and, sometimes, that entails reaching out for help.

In an actual workshop we stay with the question even if a client were to describe an "impossible" solution, such as a deceased person being alive, and we acknowledge that wish and then ask "how would that make a difference in your life?" Then as the client describes that he/she might feel as if they have their companion back, again, we ask "how would that make a difference?" With that, the client may say, "I would have someone to confide in and support me." From there, we would ask the client to think of others in their life who could begin to be a confidant in a very small manner.

CONCEPT OF CHANGE

If you are struggling with the concept of change, these questions catapult you from a problem-saturated context into a visionary context where you have a moment of freedom so as to step out of your problem story and into a story where you are more problem free. But, more importantly, it helps you identify exactly what you really want.

Even if it is only a question of surviving thus far, that alone is evidence of personal strengths and skills which you can mobilize in the future.

This is important: visionary questioning means to ask questions as a Philosopher and answer as a Visionary.

Please remember this: Your mind is capable of performing many powerful tasks, and the most powerful is its ability to create concepts because concepts become perceptions and – to your mind – perception is reality. In many instances, if your mind can conceive it, your mind and body can achieve it.

From concept to perception to achievement only requires that you take action… after you've made a plan and established the resources necessary to at least allow you to start. Once you've started on a path you really want to follow you will always find a way to get whatever you need to continue on.

I recommend the following approach:

- Do whatever it takes to develop an 'attitude of gratitude'. The more you recognize and express gratitude for the things you have, the more things you will have to express gratitude for. Without gratitude, happiness is rare. With gratitude, the odds for happiness go up dramatically. Giving thanks brings joy. You and I can find all kinds of things for which we can give thanks.
- According to some people who are very committed to the value of creating an attitude of gratitude, they follow a 5 point guideline:

1) write it down
2) talk about it
3) meditate
4) express it

5) seek it

Successful people practice gratitude. And I'm not just referring to financial success. After all, how can you be truly successful if you aren't happy and thankful for all life has to offer?

If you're interested in learning more about Attitudes of Gratitude, check out our website (www.dynamicdiscovery.ca) for a free download on the topic.

THE SPEEDOMETER

If you had trouble completing the "magic" questions, the following exercise will provide a different approach.

Settle yourself in a comfortable chair and, with your eyes closed, take several deep breaths and, as you do, imagine that you are breathing in a sense of wellness and calm and exhaling any unwanted or uncomfortable feelings.

And now, see for yourself what it would be like if you <u>could</u> slow down your world long enough to make any decisions necessary to help you through this exercise.

For instance: If you are a "road-rager", what if you could slow your world down long enough to see yourself at the wheel – always safe and always secure - and notice that the speedometer is registering "100" and as you watch it begins to reduce, going from 100 to 90 to 80 to 70 to 60 to 50 – and you're still safe and secure but your entire body is slowing down too – and the speedometer is now at 40 then down to 30 to 20 to 10 – and now you see and feel it as it goes to 9, 8, 7, 6, 5, 4… and 3… and 2… and 1… and stop… and let go… and relax… and see what you are going to do to <u>begin</u> to solve the problem.

And now you are relaxed and calm and ready to move forward – watch as the speedometer moves from 0 to 1 to 10 to 20 to 30 to 40 to 50 to 60 to 70 to 80 to 90 and back to 100. And safe and steady.

Now you can see clearly the first step you are going to take in order to <u>begin</u> to solve the problem.

HOW THE MIND WORKS

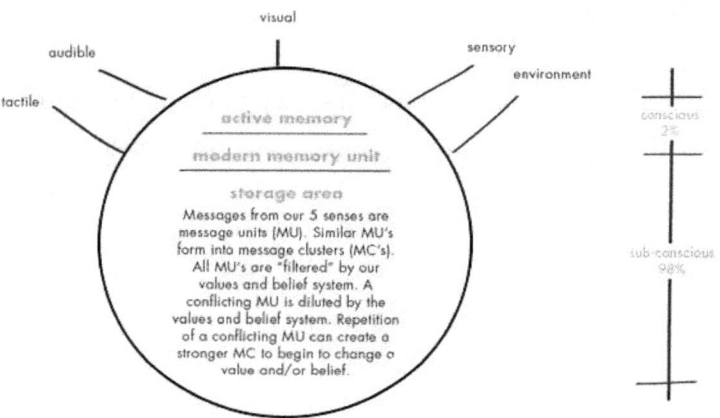

Belief Systems
Initially established by:
-culture
-religion
-authority figures

We change our belief systems through repetition --- change a habit practicing another habit until it is stronger. Experiential learning is stronger than theoretical.

Purpose of the Mind
-assess and evaluate
-decide (form judgments)
-instruct the brain
-storage of memory units

Every experience, action, thought, observation is stored

forever in the subconscious portion of the mind. The Primitive Memory holds the fight or flight response.

As shown, message units (MU's) enter the Active / Conscious portion of the mind from all 5 sources. MU's *"download"* from the Active / Conscious into the Modern Memory Unit portion of the mind on a regular basis, say every 1 ½ hours (sometimes more, sometimes less), and are held in Modern Memory for up to 24 hours then they download into the Storage portion of the mind.

Similar message units form clusters which are stronger than a single MU. In order to overcome a cluster (belief system) that is causing us problems we must strengthen another message unit through repetition until it forms a cluster stronger than the old (unwanted) cluster. For instance, you are told over and over for most of your formative, impressionable, life that you are no good, stupid and will never amount to anything. At age 30, 40 or 50 your life sort of proves this out. You keep sabotaging anything of value. You want to change. How do you go about it?

First, think back to the discussion about changing your thinking through changing programs and through looking at the <u>reality</u> of the situation. Reality, not some fantasy projection. Write out the particulars of the situation. We write it out because our mind is capable of tricking us. Seeing your thoughts on paper is real.

Second, once the reality is uncovered it needs to be acknowledged until it becomes the strong, dominant message.

Third, what you want to become must also be based on reality. Repetition (practice) allows us to become what we are capable of becoming.

PUNISHMENT OR REWARD?

How do we turn (apparent) punishment into an (apparent) reward?

A task or project we dread (a punishment) can become okay (a reward) if we break it down into manageable "bites" and determine what the benefit (reward) will be when we complete the task or project.

For Instance

In my work I must, from time-to-time, call upon people who owe money to the organization and are overdue on their payment. I dislike this task (a punishment) and often procrastinate until my boss gets annoyed with me. Then I do it, but I do not enjoy any part of it. And I resent my boss, even though it is part of my duties, and our relationship is strained.

What is the reality here? Reality is that the unpaid amount is owing for a service that our organization performed at the clients' request. The client, by not paying, has broken the agreement that we have honored. The client is the problem, not our organization. To allow the client to "get away" with this inappropriate behavior is to imply approval, which makes it easier for the client to "stiff" other organizations. And that would be wrong.

By holding the client responsible for their own actions I am, in fact, helping them to learn a valuable lesson which, in the fullness of time, may keep them out of serious trouble. Therefore I am <u>not</u> their enemy here -- even though they may choose to see me as such, and even if others agree with that assessment. Reality is my truth!

What is my reward? My reward is that the work (collecting unpaid accounts) is important to my organizations' survival. And, since I derive economic benefit (my pay cheque) from my organization, it is in my Best Interest to ensure that all accounts are paid. So, through the performance of the dreaded collection activities, I am serving my own Best Interest.

What about the delinquent client? If I approach the collection task as a matter of honoring a contract, then I may be able to stick to the reality of the situation and not get anxious or angry, or in some way attack the client. And, I will be more likely to <u>not</u> get hooked into the clients' inappropriate behavior. The client may learn a valuable lesson, and they will get that lesson without having engaged in emotional hostile actions.

RELATIONSHIPS AND BEHAVIOR

The surest way to bring people into your circle (closer to you) <u>may be</u> to attract them in through behavior changes.

<u>IF</u> Self = Best Interest,
then who is the best person to look
after <u>your</u> best interest?

For these purposes, best interest is defined as <u>not</u> being deliberately hurtful or harmful to self <u>or</u> others.

We operate as a *"smart system"* that is capable of evaluating for our needs and determining what to do in order to meet those needs. Once we build our library of activities and events that will help us meet our needs our *"smart system"* will evaluate and choose the best option(s).

Because no other person can live my life for me, it follows that I am the one person on this planet who can restore my own dignity and self-respect. No one else can do that for me.

RELATIONSHIPS CIRCLE

"BALANCED"

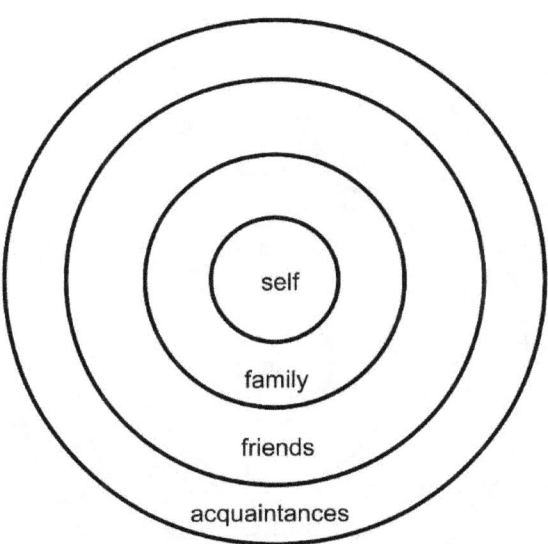

This "Balanced" chart depicts what would be considered an ideal relationship circle, with you at the center and next would be your family members followed by friends and then acquaintances.

The following "Unbalanced" chart is used to illustrate an unwanted relationship circle (unwanted but actual) that shows a dysfunctional relationship state.

"UNBALANCED"

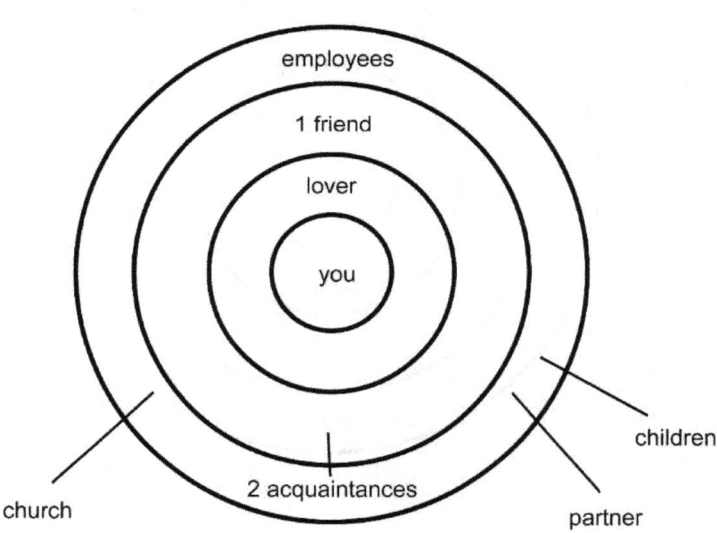

RELATIONSHIPS AND NEEDS

We always strive to meet our 5 basic needs (LAFFS):

1. Love and belonging

2. Achievement, power, recognition

3. Freedom

4. Fun

5. Survival

In this process we only evaluate for the first 4 needs, since our presence here acknowledges that our Survival need has already been met. When evaluating the ways that we use to meet our needs we can determine whether it is the activity or the people, or both, that is need fulfilling.

We can use an activity or relationship to meet more than one need, and we can evaluate how to meet our needs to a greater extent. That puts us in control of how much quality we have in our life and how to get it.

When a relationship fails to meet our needs we may find, upon evaluation, that a selection error has occurred or that the relationship <u>never</u> met one of our basic needs --- maybe it was a relationship based upon guilt or dependency or enabling, rather than being based upon a *"need"* connection.

Relationships and Needs

"BALANCED"

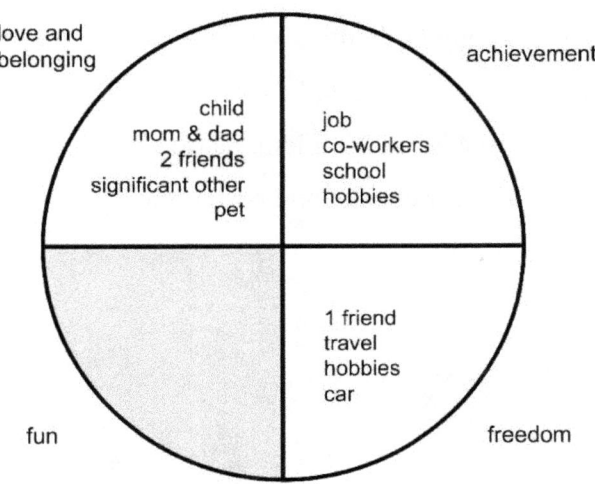

"UNBALANCED"

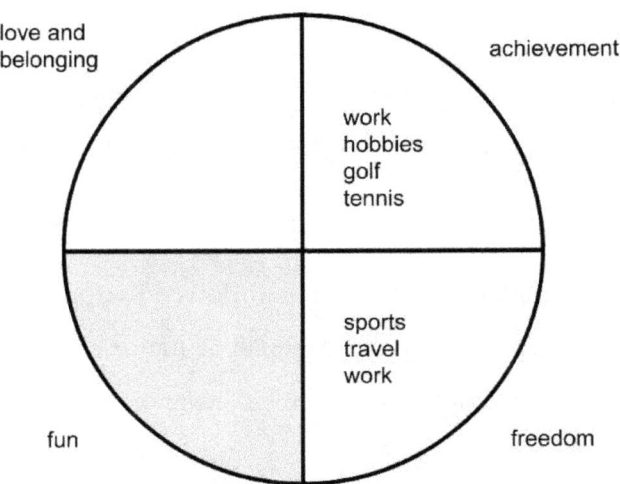

CONTROL CAR

This car is front wheel drive. The brain is the engine and the mind is the steering wheel. We are a total behavioral system. The human body is a very smart system that has never been fully duplicated. No other living thing has the power of thought and implementation that a human has, nor the ability for change and correction.

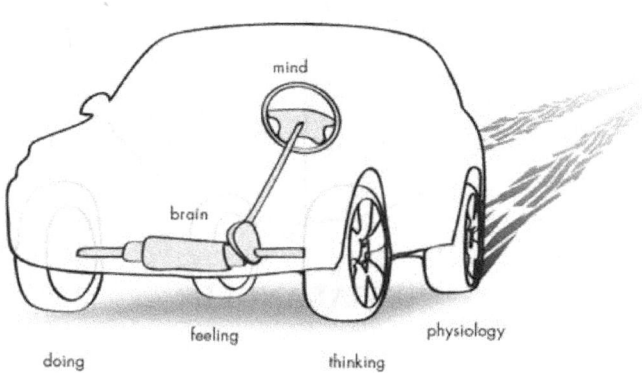

A car like the one pictured above, with well-balanced *"tires"*, will drive you properly in the direction you want to go.

First there is a thought which is followed by feelings, actions and physiological response. A major elevation in any of the behaviors would have the same effect as greatly overinflating that particular *"tire"*. Repression of the behavior deflates the particular *"tire"*.

In the example shown below the thinking *"tire"* is obsessive (greatly inflated), the feelings are *"somewhat"* inflated, and the actions are *"somewhat"* deflated (one becomes less active). Done long enough and your health (physiology) could suffer. This car would not steer well --- it wouldn't be taking you in the direction you want to go.

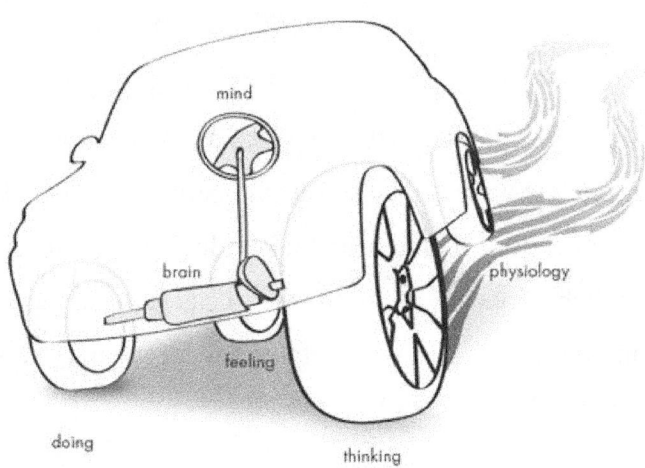

CONTROL COMPUTER

We are a total behavioral system. The human body is a very smart system that has never been duplicated. No other living thing has the power of thought and implementation that a human has, nor the ability for change and correction.

The way to change how we think is to change our thinking with a new *"program"*. Since all change is stressful it is comforting to know that the old program will always be on our *"hard drive"* (in our memory) allowing us the choice between old and new programs. If, at any time we want to revisit our old behaviors we just have to access our memory and take a look. As well, if the new behaviors are too extreme we can replace them with another new program -- totally new or we may want to balance or blend them.

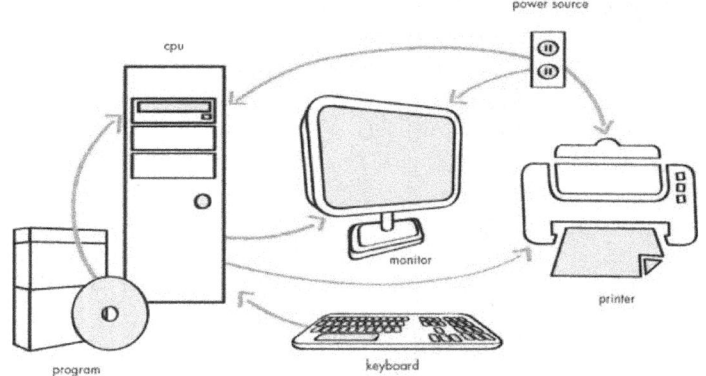

With the computer the keyboard represents our thoughts and the monitor represents our mind, which forms judgments. A computers' *"judgments"* are saved in the memory of one or more drive, while ours are saved in our minds' memory. With the computer, entering a print command is taking the action attached to the thought.

If you key information into a computer whose program is not compatible with that information the computer will either produce garbage (bizarre behaviors) or it will reject it (contrary belief systems). To process it properly the computer will need a new program.

GOAL SETTING

What Can Be Done? Are there steps the individual can take?

Setting Goals

You must be realistic and honest with yourself. If you set goals that you can't possibly reach, you are setting yourself up for failure. You will make yourself frustrated and unhappy. The key here is a realistic and honest assessment of your potential.

Be wary of making otherwise perfectly reasonable goals unattainable because of stringent time frames. When you set a goal, you will most likely set times for achieving certain steps along your way to achieving your final goal. Even if you don't set the time frames formally, you will probably have a pretty good idea of how long you are giving yourself. It's wise to sit down and formally set these goals. Think about it and give yourself reasonable time to achieve them. Make a deal with yourself to view these time limits as flexible.

Don't get discouraged if things don't work out as planned. Sometimes finding our place takes both time and error. All of us experience failures of one magnitude or another. The key is to view the failures as a learning experience - if nothing else, failures teach us what not to do. Remain flexible. As long as you keep focusing on your strengths and potential, the right thing will come along - and probably sooner rather than later. But don't quit at the first sign of boredom. Even if you have truly found your niche, you will not feel enthusiastic 100 percent of the time.

Don't worry about others - don't compare your progress with that of others. Focus on your own achievements. Work to develop your skills and talents to their full potential. Compete with yourself – your short term goals should be based on today's accomplishments. If you have reached Point A today, make Point B your next objective - improve yourself and don't worry about the other guy.

Define exactly what you want to do. Define a reasonable time frame. Know what you have to do to get there. You don't need to know every little detail, but you do have to have the big picture and many of the details.

If you have a goal in mind but don't know what it takes to reach it, then you need to find out. Do some reading, talk to people who know, ask questions and LISTEN to the answers. Think that sounds like a lot of work? Well, remember what you are preparing for; your success and happiness. A little research into what it will take for you to reach your goals isn't too difficult.

LIVE UP TO YOUR GREATEST POTENTIAL

Your success depends upon your will and capability to live to your full potential. If you want to make more of your talents and live up to your full potential, you have to learn to use them.

What makes a high achiever? Is it luck, intelligence, talent, dedication? All of these things figure in; they all make a difference. But we all know intelligent, talented, hard-working people who do not consider themselves very successful or even happy. And we know people who are not exceptionally bright but seem happy and successful. So there must be something else, some secret to success. Actually there are several secrets to achieving your peak performance, to living up to your full potential.

Your success at business, friendship, love, sports -- just about anything you try -- is largely determined by your own self-image. Your unhappiness is something you choose.

Say what?

I know. I know that you're thinking, "Hey! No one chooses to be unhappy."

Well, maybe not -- but you have to consciously choose to be happy, self-confident, and successful. Happiness is elusive when we go after it directly. As is self-confidence.

Happiness and self-confidence both seem to be more "side-products" than something you can achieve in and for itself. So how, then, can consciously choosing to be these things be of any value? Well, the secret is to focus on other things.

FOCUS ON YOUR POTENTIAL

First, focus on your potential. Begin by making a complete and accurate assessment of your potential. To do this you must take an inventory of yourself. Then, go back to the list of things you can do well.

Complete the personal inventory questionnaire at the end of this document. Once completed, go to your list of things you like to do but you feel you don't do well. Next, go to your list of things you would like to do if you could.

Ask yourself, "Why can't I do this, if I'd like to?" Put your reasons on another list. You have just made an assessment of yourself. Look over your lists again. You are focusing on all the things you feel you can't do and the reasons why you can't do them, right? Well, don't.

FOCUS ON WHAT YOU CAN DO

FOCUS ON YOUR POTENTIAL

Make it a habit to focus on your strengths. Don't forget to include your undeveloped potential, as well. Train yourself to focus on your potential instead of your limitations. That's not to say that you should ignore your list of reasons for not doing some of the things you would like to do. But look at them from the viewpoint of your strengths.

Find Your Strengths

You see the difference? Focusing on your limitations lets those limitations make your decisions for you. Focusing on your strengths lets YOU make the decision. When you've decided to overcome your limitations to do something you really want to do you will be more determined to develop your strengths to compensate. You will do well, because you will be doing what you really want to do and you will be determined to develop the full potential of your strengths. Very few people concentrate on fully developing any of their strengths. That's where you will have the edge. You know your true disadvantages but your determination, your singleness of purpose, will inspire you to fully develop the talents and skills you do have.

Go to your assessment of yourself:

- What do you have a major interest in?
  _____

- What do you have a natural aptitude for?
  _____

Go for it:

- Devote yourself to something you really like to do.
- Don't choose something just because you think you could make more money at it than you could by doing something else that you would really rather work at. You won't work to develop your full potential.
- You may start out with enthusiasm, but you will soon raise the flag. It will be a chore to go to work. You'll probably find yourself hating to go.
- It'll be difficult to work on improving your skills because you don't like what you are doing. You probably won't be working up to your potential.
- Your success will probably be limited by your growing lack of interest and your happiness will surely be affected.

If, however, you devote yourself to something you really like to do, you'll enjoy your work, you'll be enthusiastic, and you'll probably find yourself working on improving your skills just for the sheer joy of it. You will be working to reach your full potential. You'll probably soon find you are making more money at this truly interesting occupation than you ever dreamed possible. And because you like what you are doing, you will be happier. When you know you are working to your full potential and you enjoy your work and begin to feel successful, you will find that self-confidence and happiness soon follow.

The Benefit of Research

Train yourself into making this "research" the next focus of your life.

You will be focusing on your strengths, on your purpose, and on learning and doing. If you have chosen a goal that is right for you, focusing on these things and devoting the necessary time should not be too difficult. It may take a bit of self-discipline at first, but your determination and interest will carry you through until the focusing process becomes a habit.

When you have a real desire to accomplish something, initiative should only require an occasional shove -- but you may need to give it a nudge now and again.

FUTURIZING

(HAVING OUR WORLD THE WAY WE WANT IT TO BE)

Purpose:

> To identify the needs we are controlling for. It is not designed to resolve issues; it **is** designed to <u>start</u> meeting needs.

Plan:

> 1) If your world was the way you wanted it, 5 years from now, what would it "look" like? What would you be thinking, doing, feeling?
> 2) Writing it out is more effective and hooks into our beliefs.

Criteria:

> 1) Not dependent on anyone else to make it happen.
> 2) Occurs five years in the future.
> 3) Takes place on <u>this</u> planet.
> 4) For general audiences only. (not sexually explicit)

The purpose is to identify what needs we are controlling for.

<u>Evaluation</u>:
1) Look for the <u>energy</u> and the needs being met by the futurizing exercise.
2) This exercise is a way to get permission to enter the new world being envisioned.
3) What would you be thinking, doing and feeling if your world was exactly the way you wanted it to be?

DGS

(DARN GOOD START)

This is where we get to working out solutions and finding ways to start experiencing some victories and to start building more quality into our lives. Remember, we do not evaluate for right and wrong, or for good and bad. What is, is, and what ain't, ain't. You can't be measured by someone else's yardstick.

<u>Criteria</u>:
1) Must be easy to do and not doing now.
2) Must be something we <u>want</u> to do.
3) Must be tangible, reportable and timely (48 to 72 hrs).
4) Doing it once is rewarding.
5) Continuing to do DGS's will <u>help</u> meet the need.
6) It must address the <u>need</u> rather than the <u>want</u>.

This is our prescription for meaningful change. Continuous and constant application conditions us to structure winning and control in our lives. We always use LAFFS to determine what we are DGS'ing for:

1) Are you interested in finding something else to that will get you what you really want? If you <u>don't</u> know, do a futurizing exercise to find the need(s) you want to satisfy.

2) The action might involve just making a list of things we might like to do and aren't doing now.

3) Define your expectation of a DGS, and what a DGS would look like to you.

4) You must understand and deal with the way things really are.

5) Is it safe?

THE PROCESS
(*FOR GETTING WHAT YOU REALLY WANT*)

What **do** you really want from life? More money? A happy marriage? A new home? Fame? Success? Whatever it is, it is possible for you to have it. No matter whether it seems impossible right now. Imagine the life of your dreams…and make it come true. Harness your own power of positive thinking, stress management, instinct and above all, commitment.

You can learn how to conceive, believe and achieve the goals you truly desire. With an open mind and dedication, you will quickly learn how to literally have everything you want. Get the insight and knowledge you need to reach your goals.

To get started you don't have to study anything, meet anyone, go anywhere. You don't have to **do** anything. All that is required of you is an open mind. The principle is based on your ability to:

- Conceive
- Believe

- Achieve

The principle will always work for those who maintain an open mind and are willing to do <u>anything</u> to achieve <u>their</u> goal.

THE LAW OF THE OPEN MIND ALLOWS THINGS TO WORK WITHOUT INTERFERENCE

To make this "Secret" work for you, you will need just two things:

1. A clear idea of what you want -- a clear objective. The clear idea is necessary because your mind needs definition, time and dimension – sharp, clear and specific.

2. Commitment – defined as a feeling of confidence, a firm belief that you will do <u>anything</u> to get it.

You <u>don't</u> need:

1. A plan of action

2. Money

3. Time

4. Luck

5. Special intelligence
6. Help from others
7. Special education

The principle of the secret is a natural built-in mechanism that most of us lose as we build our biases -- which usually come from someone else and form our belief systems. Fix the image clearly in your mind and lock it there. Know <u>precisely</u> what you want. You can't have it if you don't know what it "looks" like.

For example:

- You want to be a millionaire. Why? For what purpose? What will $1 million <u>do</u> for you?
- Want to be happy? What is it that makes you happy?

Understand how it works. I mean, <u>really</u> understand how it works by writing out in detail the answers to the above-noted questions. In great detail!

Objective and Commitment are everything. Have willingness. Have the willingness to do <u>anything</u> to get it.

HOW IT WORKS

1) CONCEPT. Willingness is a concept. Concept is a thought. It can't be seen, touched or proved. Love is a thought and a feeling. Thought is also a <u>physical</u> reality. Form your thoughts and let them move to reality.

2) LAW. The law of attraction says "things" attract other "things". Gravitation is the mutual attraction of any two bodies.
Whenever you have a thought it begins to attract its <u>physical</u> equivalent. When you think about being hungry you begin to get hungry. If there is food around you will soon be eating. Think about being sad and you will soon be sad. Think about being thirsty and before you know it you are thirsty. Positive attitude programs all preach the same message -- to win you must think about winning. To succeed, you must think of what success is for you. What the human mind can conceive and believe, the human mind and body can achieve. The thought of winning attracts the <u>physical</u> counterpart to winning, as does the thought of success, etc.

3) PHENOMENON. Thinking of $10 million <u>begins</u> to attract that money to you. Time is the key factor. The phenomenon is known as "accelerating acceleration" --- it moves faster once it is started, if there is commitment and willingness to do anything required. Thinking is nice but goes nowhere on its own; you need to get into action! Every self-made millionaire will tell you that the time required to earn the first million was more than for the second million, and so on. AS LONG AS the commitment and willingness remain.

4) POWER (of an open mind). This is a mysterious power. Most people choose <u>not</u> to understand it. Most people already have their minds made up. Closed on life's major issues, they would rather not be bothered with changing them. The law of an open mind allows things to work without interference.

   An open mind allows the law of accelerating acceleration to run free. When you keep your mind open, you allow your thoughts to find their physical equivalents a closed mind would not have thought possible -- and with a speed a closed mind would not have thought possible.

An open mind is what makes everything else work. The Concept, the Law, the Phenomenon, the Power -- the very principle, itself.

The principle embodied herein will work whether you are aware of it or not. Just as we can ignite the Principle's power we can also defuse it. There is something that keeps the Principle from working, and it is insidious. For instance, you want to become the President of your company within 5 years. You understand you must be willing to do anything to get it. You make a list of the process and find there are 45 items (or steps) involved in the objective. You must work in all departments; you must work 12 hours per day, 6 days per week; and so on. Until you reach item 42 which is a move to the corporate headquarters. But, you don't want to leave your current situation -- you love your community and friends, etc. BANG! The door is slamming shut before you even begin to walk through it. You have become unwilling before you even start.

Maybe you should just start working through the items on your list. If you find out that you do not want to commit to the objective anymore -- because you didn't have a clear understanding of what was entailed -- you can investigate your "needs" further and find an objective that you will be willing to do anything for.

Murphy's Law says that if something can stop this process it will. Because of lack of definition and understanding. If you set a goal and find that there is something you are unwilling to do, save yourself the trouble. Forget that goal and start looking elsewhere.

There are endless worthy goals in the universe. There is one made for you.

The opposite side of Murphy's Law says that when you become committed – absolutely clear in your mind and willing to do whatever it takes to achieve your goal – the Principle goes to work creating short cuts, eliminating items from your list. Accelerating acceleration. You must be willing to do everything necessary because you do not know which items will be eliminated. If one item is unacceptable then the whole idea is unacceptable.

You may want to be a doctor. You can't be a doctor unless you are willing to take "doctor" training. All of it. You must be willing to do it all. That is it, and that is all.

You never know how it will come about, but you must start the process, work at it, and watch it unfold.

STAY COMMITTED!

It is not about doing all of the tasks. It is about your <u>willingness</u> to do all of the tasks that gets the Principle going. You don't even have to know all of the tasks if you are committed to the objective and willing to do whatever it takes. Willingness will lead you into the "flow", and being committed will keep you in the flow.

An open mind will provide the directions.

HOWEVER, there is a danger in accomplishing goals! Accomplished goals have a certain tyranny in them:

> - if accomplishment is your only goal in life you will never be satisfied with achieving your goals. You will be like an addict, an accomplishment junkie always having to go after another goal. Or,

> - having achieved your goal you may feel a sense of loss and give up because the attainment of a goal never measures up to the expectation.

There are endless examples of athletes, movie stars, entrepreneurs (whiz kids), etc, who attain their pinnacle early and then turn to destructive things like drugs, or other non-productive obsessions.

The trick is, once you attain your goal, change it up or move to another field and start over. Create a new beginning and a new excitement. Keep doing and progressing.

LOVE WHAT YOU SET OUT TO ACHIEVE AND FOLLOW YOUR PASSION

If you want to be an Olympic sprinter you had better <u>love</u> running sprints, because that is what you will be doing. Day in and day out. For years. And years.

Now – just to keep you off-balance – here is something else to consider:

What if all your problems are just memories?

When I first heard that question I'll admit I was stumped. Thankfully I kept an open mind and I'm glad to tell you the question now makes sense, and it can become a powerful method for re-training ourselves to stay present and detached from past behavior patterns that can cause a lot of damage in all areas of our lives.

Think of a problem that you used to believe you had (notice how we purposely phrase the question in the past tense). If you are having a hard time accepting that the problem is behind you, include every moment that has passed *as part of the past*.

You just have to think of the past as anything that is not happening *right now* and you will see what choices are available to you with clear eyes.

Because this is likely a big change in your thinking, it requires conscious effort to make it a familiar response. If you're no longer tied to the mistakes of your past then you're free to make decisions based on reason and you'll always be centered enough to *respond*, rather than *react*. This approach teaches you to remember how you *used* to behave in a certain way, so that you can finally let go of behaving that way out of habit.

It may sound bizarre, but it works. And, it's enlightening. So many of the things we used to believe about ourselves don't have to hold true anymore; not if we don't want them to. So that voice in your head that used to say, "I *always* pick the wrong stock," or "I'm *always* late for important stuff," doesn't need to be true right now. That can be the old story.

That was then, this is now; that's the root of this new way of thinking that challenges us to take responsibility by seeing that we actually *create* our problems by expecting them. If we believe that we have a problem then we focus on whatever validates that belief.

CONCLUSION

Now that you have completed the Destiny in Motion process I'd like to assure you that this process is by no means a new concept. In fact, a similar process was discussed by Napoleon Hill, a prolific writer who produced a series of books called 'Philosophy of Achievement', some 30 volumes and all with a consistent message: Success.

The truly amazing thing is that Hill's first book was written in 1925, is still available today, and has sold over 20 million copies.

Hill considered freedom, democracy, capitalism, and harmony to be important contributing elements to this philosophy. Hill claimed throughout his writings that without these foundations upon which to build, successful personal achievements were not possible. He contrasted his philosophy with others' and thought that the Achievement Philosophy was superior. He felt that it was responsible for the success Americans enjoyed for the better part of two centuries. Negative emotions such as fear, selfishness, etc., had no part to play in his philosophy.

Hill considered those emotions to be the source of failure for unsuccessful people

Hill tantalized his readers by referring to the secret of success through analogy, such as: *If you truly desire money so keenly that your desire is an obsession, you will have no difficulty in convincing yourself that you will acquire it. The object is to want money, and to be so determined to have it that you convince yourself that you will have it. However, you can never have riches in great quantities unless you work yourself into a white heat of desire for money, and actually believe you will possess it.* Do not presume it is this which is the secret that Hill refers to, but the definition of the 'secret' is far more effective if realized by the reader when they are ready for it.

Napoleon Hill eventually resolved the secret at the end of his book 'The Law of Success'; it is the <u>Golden Rule</u>. Only by working harmoniously in co-operation with other individuals or groups of individuals and thus creating value and benefit for them will one create sustainable achievement for oneself.

You see, what Hill wanted to do to his readers and students — which I don't, of course, want to do to you — was to find some way of motivating them to be congruent and expressive in their behavior at all times and as creative as they could be as human beings. He wanted them to mobilize their resources so that each act that they performed would be a full representation of all the potential that was available to them — all the personal power that they had that was available to them at any moment in time.

Borrowing from 'The Teachings of don Juan' by Carlos Castenada, during their travels together Juan was educating Carlos about the realities of life. Specifically what Juan, a Yaqui Indian, told Carlos was "At any moment that you find yourself hesitating, or if at any moment you find yourself putting off until tomorrow trying some new piece of behavior that you could do today, or doing something you've done before, then all you need to do is glance over your left shoulder and there will be a fleeting shadow. That shadow represents your death, and at any moment it might step forward, place its hand on your shoulder and take you. So, that act that you are presently engaged in might be your very last act and therefore fully representative of you as your last act on this planet."

One of the ways you can use this advice constructively is to understand that it is indulgent to hesitate. When you hesitate, you are acting as though you are immortal. You are not.

You don't even know the place and the hour of your death.

And so one thing you can do – to remind yourself that not to bother to hesitate is not to act unprofessional – is to just suddenly glance over your left shoulder and remember that death is standing there, and make death your advisor. And know that he or she will always tell you to do something representative of your full potential as a person. You can afford no less.

Now, that's a little bit heavy. That's why I wouldn't tell that to you. But I will offer you an alternative: If at any point you discover yourself hesitating, or being incongruent, or putting off until tomorrow something you could try now, or just needing some new choices, or being bored, glance over your right shoulder and there I will be, urging you on.

And reminding you that any questions you might have can be self-answered through the use of the magic question.

As a reminder, the magic question goes like this:

Suppose our meeting is over, you go home, do whatever you planned to do for the rest of the day. And then, sometime in the evening, you get tired and go to sleep. And in the middle of the night, when you are fast asleep, a miracle happens and all the problems that brought you here today are solved... just like that. But since the miracle happened overnight nobody is telling you that the miracle happened. When you wake up the next morning, how are you going to start discovering that the miracle happened?

_____

_____

What else are you going to notice?

_____

_____

And that's just one way that your subconscious can make sense of, and deal with, all the material that it has absorbed during the Dynamic Discovery program.

A Note For You…

- Nothing in the world is a gift; whatever it is you have has been, in some way, worked for.
- Whatever there is to learn has to be learned the hard way.
- Turn the Destiny in Motion concepts into a viable way of life by a process of repetition.
- Everything new in our lives, such as the Destiny in Motion concepts, must be repeated to us to the point of exhaustion before we open ourselves to it.

And that's how you go about getting what you really, really, <u>really</u> want from your life.

Personal Inventory Guide

To do a personal self-inventory of your life, ask yourself these simple but life-exposing questions:

- Are you generally happy?
- Are you generally sad?
- Do you feel free or do you feel trapped?
- Are you content or are you stressed?
- Do you live with joy and love or do you live with sadness and fear?
- Are you holding on to pain from the past, or have you taken time to let go, heal, and move forward?
- Are you in a healthy, harmonious relationship, or are you in a relationship that is full of turmoil, regret, and sadness?
- Is your life in balance, or are you living from one dramatic episode to another?
- Do you hold resentment or do you have forgiveness?
- Do you live with trust, or do you live in fear that somehow those around you will do you harm?
- How is your self-image?

- Do you like what you see when you look in the mirror?
- Do you feel healthy and fit, or do you live as a victim of illness?
- Do you have dreams and goals that you are striving for, or do you just live day to day, allowing whatever shows up to form your life?
- Do you appreciate all that you have around you, or do you take your positive circumstances for granted?
- Do you give back to those less fortunate, or do you hold on to your possessions tightly and believe in scarcity?
- Do you have self-love?

Now, there's only one other thing left to do... and that is to say Goodbye and wish you a Good Life. Please leave a review by scanning this link back to Amazon.

RESOURCES

Credit for much of my base of knowledge belongs to:
- The Alandel School and Clinic (hypnotherapy training).
- 20 years experience working as a counselor and employee assistance program manager for Human Resources Services Ltd. (HRS).
- The Heartview Foundation of Mandan, North Dakota, where I learned about addictions.
- 26 years of immersion in the program of Alcoholics Anonymous.
- 25 years of studying various programs/approaches such as NLP, Psychology, Cognitive Behavioural Therapy, Quantum Physics and Reality Therapy.
- Abraham Maslow's hierarchy of needs.
- Dr. William Glasser, a psychiatrist who developed Reality Therapy / Control Theory and is the father of Reality Therapy and Control Theory and is also founder of the Reality Therapy Institute.
- The writings of Milton Erickson which drew upon his own experiences to provide examples of the power of the unconscious mind. He was largely

self-taught.
- Dave Elman, who was self-taught and wrote "Hypnotherapy" which was self-published.
- The book Alcoholics Anonymous (commonly known as The Big Book), the members I've come to know and love both in AA and its sister organization, Alanon.
- The teachings of Socrates, especially those concerning inductive reasoning (to draw logical conclusions) and his Four basic Principles of Philosophy.
- The writings of Napoleon Hill, who enjoyed a long and successful career writing, teaching, lecturing about the principles of success, and whose work is still relevant for those seeking personal achievement and motivation.
- The writings of Carlos Castaneda – particularly The Teachings of Don Juan – who was an American author with a Ph. D in anthropology
- Tony Robbins - The Six Human Needs.
- Manfred Max-Neef (along with Antonio Elizalde and Martin Hopenhayn) developed the theory of Human Needs and Human-Scale Development.

Personal

Prior to developing the DYNAMIC DISCOVERY process I was presenting and leading a two day seminar program - I called *"THE PERSONAL IMPROVEMENT SERIES"* - that consisted of 4 topics, each of which were 4 hours in duration, typically presented on Saturday and Sunday. The 4 topics were: Intimate Relationships; Guilt; Co-Dependency, and; The Right To Choose and were sponsored by an Employee and Family Assistance Program (EFAP) provider who had contracts to provide psychological counseling services to various corporations and government agencies.

I worked with several groups of clients from whom I learned some things that were never on my agenda. I did not want to be a counselor or therapist, and I certainly did not want to be anyone's advisor; I just enjoyed presenting information to people who were interested in looking at ways to make changes in their lives. Those first clients lead me into this process of self-evaluation through their enthusiastic and active participation which turned my seminars (or workshops) into participatory group sessions.

The basis for my foundation book came about in December, 1995, while I was sorting my notes from 4 years of those group sessions because I wanted to create a document that could be used by some of my clients who wanted to understand the *"hows"* and *"whys"* of the process that unfolded during those group sessions. There is no way that I had the knowledge or training to – on my own – develop the DYNAMIC DISCOVERY process; it came from real life situations and the very real people who shared their thoughts and stories with the Group and who allowed me to learn from them and keep some notes on what was happening during those early sessions because the process works through the group members and not through the group leader. The notes have never been used for reports to employers or others persons outside the Group and for reasons of respect and confidentiality real client names have not been used. Because this is a <u>self-evaluation</u> process there are no experts or gurus; all I know that my clients don't know is the progression of the process and what the next question will be. I am not an expert or a guru - just someone privileged to share information that other non-experts have provided to me, in a format that a broad range of people can easily grasp and understand.

"Dynamic Discovery is a personal development process that will lead you to an understanding of how to take control of your life ... again."

Our positive and relaxed atmosphere enables our members to use the group process to make effective and meaningful changes in their individual lives. We combine a supportive, non-critical group environment with an innovative process for personal change.

Discover how to get started on getting what you really want from life. Discover how to move from unwanted behaviours to wanted behaviours.

Discover how to regain control of your life and how to achieve balance in all aspects (mental /physical / spiritual).

Discover how to improve your personal image. Discover how to make gain without pain.

Discover how to deal with personal issues, such as:

Marital/relationship problems.
Pre-marital counsel.
Moving past a "stuck – point".
Weight / fitness management.
Relapse prevention (addictions).
Declining work performance.
Corporate downsizing ("outplacement").
Early retirement.
Sexual / physical abuse.
And any other thinking, feeling, or doing problems humans can have. Dynamic Discovery is a process of self-evaluation, based upon getting what you want and dealing with your needs.

All you need to bring with you is an open-mind.

Come on over and visit our website at www.DynamicDiscovery.ca

ABOUT THE AUTHOR
GEORGE BISSETT

George has lived and/or worked in all ten Canadian provinces and three territories, as well as having lived and/or worked in 28 of the 50 states.

He had a problem with alcohol but for more than 26 years (since September 9, 1988) he has not used intoxicants of any kind. Achieving sobriety led to his interest in human behavior and, in particular, why we humans do what we do. His interest and work in the field of human behavior eventually lead him to working for an Employee Assistance Program as both a counselor and manager as well as leading and facilitating workshops and seminars. Prior to developing the DYNAMIC DISCOVERY process he was presenting and leading a two day seminar program titled "THE PERSONAL IMPROVEMENT SERIES" that consisted of 4 topics: Intimate Relationships; Guilt; Co-Dependency, and; The Right To Choose. The back and forth interactions with those seminar clients was enthusiastic and instructive, which led him into using a process of self-evaluation and eventually turned his seminars and workshops into participatory group sessions focused on unwanted and wanted behaviors and how to move from the former to the latter.

The formal format for the Dynamic Discovery program came about in December, 1995, while he was sorting his notes from 4 years of those two day seminar sessions because he wanted to create a document that could be used by some of his clients who wanted to understand the "hows" and "whys" of the process that had unfolded during those group sessions... from real life situations and the very real people who shared their thoughts and stories with the Group and who allowed him to learn from them and keep some notes on what was happening during those early sessions.

Career Path

His first career choice was the Royal Canadian Air Force and he lucked into being part of a Para-Rescue unit. Being a Jumper appealed to his sense of adventure and pumped up his esteem because Jumpers were few and far between. However, he will admit to having feelings of superiority because the greatest danger to most Airmen and Airwomen was the possibility of a life-endangering paper cut.

He spent the next 25 years as a builder and real estate

developer as well as consulting on approximately 3 million square feet of commercial buildings; mostly hotels and casinos.

Professional Development

Certified Hypnotherapist

Certified Life skills Trainer

Certified Building Technologist

Certificate in Alternative Dispute Resolution

Professional Member, International Facility Management Association

Council of Canadian Administrative Tribunals (Administrative Law)

International Association of Industrial Accident Boards and Commissions (Adjudicative Law)

Sales and Marketing Council, Canadian Home Builders Association

Disclaimer

Copyright ©2014 George Bissett.

All rights reserved. No part of this work may be reproduced or transmitted in any form or by any means – graphic, electronic or mechanic, including photocopying, recording, taping or information storage and retrieval systems – without the prior written permission of the publisher.

In other words, PLEASE don't steal our stuff. We worked hard to prepare it. Plus, the Dynamic Discovery program is all about honesty ... and stealing is just wrong.

Limits of Liability/Disclaimer of Warranty

This material is designed for educational purposes only. The author takes no responsibility for any misappropriation of the contents stated in this e-book and thus cannot and will not be held liable for any damages incurred because of it. While the author of this book has made utmost efforts to obtain updated and accurate information contained herein, the author and/or the publisher of the book cannot be held liable for any damage or loss caused by the content of this book. The author of the book does not warranty the accuracy of the contents and disclaims all warranties with respect to the information contained herein, its accuracy and applications.

The advice presented in this book may not be suitable for everyone. The information contained herein is not intended to substitute for informed medical advice or training. This book is not a substitute for professional advice and the information in this e-book should not be used to diagnose or treat a health problem. Dynamic Discovery is a process of self-evaluation. Neither the author nor the publisher of this book is engaged in rendering any professional services. If expert assistance and guidance is needed, professional help should be sought.

The author of the e-book does not endorse any person whose quotations have been used in this book. Neither the author nor the publisher of the book takes any credit for the cited quotations.

Individual results may vary.

www.ingramcontent.com/pod-product-compliance
Lightning Source LLC
Chambersburg PA
CBHW071408040426
42444CB00009B/2150